felt IMAGES

AN ALBATROSS BOOK

Contents

Introduction	4
SPLENDOUR	6
MORNING GLORY	8
APPRECIATION	10
MASTERPIECE	12
AUTUMN FESTIVAL	14
PEACE	16
REFLECTIONS	18
ARTISTRY	20
HERITAGE	22
LIVING MELODIES	24
HANDIWORK	26
BALLET	28
PLEASURE	30
ENCOURAGEMENT	32
LONELINESS	34
DEVELOPMENT	36
MATURITY	38
GROWTH	40

TRUST	42
EMPATHY	44
DIGNITY	46
INQUISITIVENESS	48
FRICTION	50
THOUGHTLESSNESS	52
SLANDER	54
SPITE	56
SORROW	58
TENDERNESS	60
CHARACTER	62
SACRIFICE	64
SAFETY	66
LIFE'S JOURNEY	68
MORNING MIST	70
SOLITUDE	72
REMINISCENCE	74
REDEMPTION	76

Introduction

When I first took these pictures, I had little idea how the silence of the images would be translated into words.

Gradually, I became aware of the images having various affects on me: sometimes they would enable a particular reality of life — beauty, joy, hurt, happiness, sorrow — to bubble up within me; at other times they would lead me to a quietness that was a reverence for the God who had made heaven and earth and all that is within it. From such feelings arose these poems.

An example of how pictures become words for me is the poem 'Sorrow'. The picture of creation I photographed seemed to capture the very depth of my feeling at the time. I had lost three close family members in an accident. They were suddenly gone and I felt very much alone. Though the years have passed, lingering tears still make their way down my cheeks. The stem of sorrow *is* fragile — sometimes I am, too.

The form of poetry used here is called haiku. Originally a Japanese verse form devised in the sixteenth century, haiku lends itself well to pithy expressions of feeling in response to pictures. The poem is composed of three lines. The first line is five syllables, the second is seven and the third is five once again — and two lines must rhyme. The total composition — picture and poem — should represent a satisfying completeness of meaning and feeling.

There is much wonder all around us — the seaside, the forests, the fern gullies, the sunsets . . . and God's hand has touched it all with colour, so beautiful, yet transparent and ever-changing. Like the seasons of our lives.

Our land is precious. I hope these felt images will enable us to see, touch and feel the beauty around us.

SPLENDOUR

Bay of azure blue,
Painted scene in pastel hue;
Harmony within.

MORNING GLORY

Image on the lake

Causes me to contemplate;

Morning's ecstasy.

APPRECIATION

Indigo, so rare,
Captured scene beyond compare;
Treasure your blessings.

MASTERPIECE

Still, the paintbrush lies,
Having painted evening skies;
Artist, talented.

AUTUMN FESTIVAL

Smiling with delight,
Autumn paints a wondrous sight;
Smile, and paint your day.

PEACE

Autumn's golden leaves,
Drifting gently on the breeze;
Peace within my soul.

REFLECTIONS

Tall and straight they stand;

Poplars, touched by Autumn's hand.

We, too, are mirrors.

ARTISTRY

Eucalyptus leaves
Brightly grace our countryside;
Silent, bushland pride.

HERITAGE

History of our land
Hidden in a gumtree's hand;
Beauty held within.

LIVING MELODIES

Waterfall cascades,
Mountain music here belongs;
Neverending songs.

HANDIWORK

Spiderweb, so new,
Sparkles with the morning dew;
Old chantilly lace.

BALLET

Clothed in purest white,
Ballerina on a tree;
Priceless sight to me.

PLEASURE

Fresh the springtime morn,
Buds awaken with the dawn;
Sunshine in my heart.

ENCOURAGEMENT

Dry, the desert plain
Comes to life with showers of rain;
Compliment a friend.

LONELINESS

Paddock, parched and dry,
Caused by nature's cloudless sky;
Emptiness within.

DEVELOPMENT

Clasped, the knotted fern
Starts to grow and slowly turn,
Reaching out to learn.

MATURITY

Spring's development,
Individuality;
Soon the growth we see.

GROWTH

Rain upon dry ground,
Sweet contentment, joys abound;
Life begins anew.

TRUST

Friends stand side by side,
Tall and straight, in honesty;
Nothing do they hide.

EMPATHY

Understanding scene;
For it shows where we have been:
Valleys and mountains.

DIGNITY

Emblem of our land
Cloaked in velvet majesty;
Regal, though in sand.

INQUISITIVENESS

Rock upon the shore,

Unbelievable design;

Fascination mine.

FRICTION

Weatherbeaten rock;
Constant pounding by time's hand
Turns it into sand.

THOUGHTLESSNESS

Unconcerned they blow,
Thistles; where they fall they grow,
Like my careless words.

SLANDER

Shape depicts the scorn,

Held within the rose's thorn;

Accusations hurt.

SPITE

Irritating weeds

Soon take root and spread their seeds:

Prickly balls of spite.

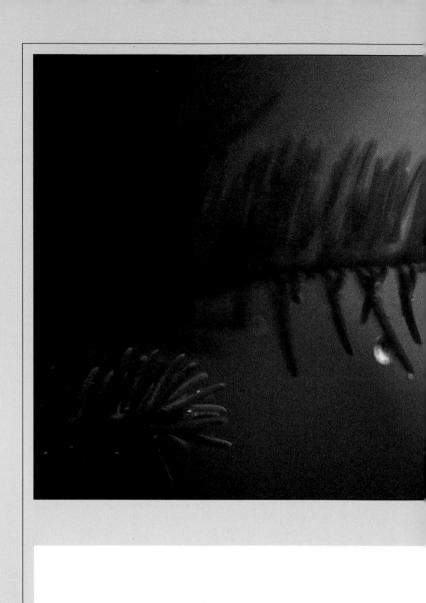

SORROW

Stem, bent low with rain,
Leaving, when the grey clouds clear,
Lingering tears.

TENDERNESS

Raindrops from above

Shroud the precious rose with love:

Nature's canopy.

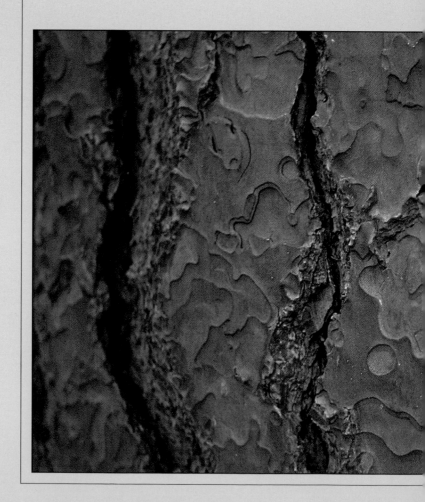

CHARACTER

Creative designs;
Underneath the bark of pines,
Hidden talents.

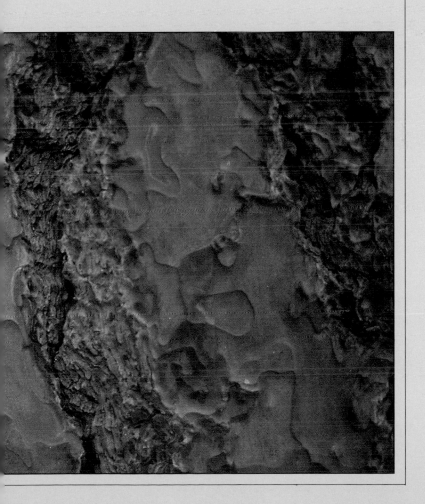

SACRIFICE

Jesus is the vine,
Making each of us a part
Of his loving heart.

SAFETY

Tiny, sun-kissed vine,
Fingers search to intertwine:
Our security.

LIFE'S JOURNEY

Misty, waking morn,
Country lane cloaked in the dawn;
Our road, too, is veiled.

MORNING MIST

Soft, the morning mist,
All of nature has been kissed;
Effervescent joy.

SOLITUDE

Soft, the evening light
Captures such a peaceful sight;
My tranquillity.

REMINISCENCE

Brilliant sunshine dies,
Leaving softly painted skies;
Memories are sweet.

REDEMPTION

Bridge, at close of day,
Links us with eternal life;
Jesus leads the way.

© Rosemary Renouf 1992

Published in Australia and New Zealand by
Albatross Books Pty Ltd
PO Box 320, Sutherland
NSW 2232, Australia
in the United States of America by
Albatross Books
PO Box 131, Claremont
CA 91711, USA
and in the United Kingdom by
Lion Publishing
Peter's Way, Sandy Lane West
Littlemore, Oxford OX4 5HG, England

First edition 1992

National Library of Australia
Cataloguing-in-Publication data

Renouf, Rosemary
Felt Images

ISBN 0 86760 162 0 (Albatross)
ISBN 0 7459 2195 7 (Lion)

I. Title

A 821.3

Design: Stephanie Cannon
Cover and all interior photographs: Rosemary Renouf
Printed and bound in Singapore by Tien Wah Press

DATE DUE